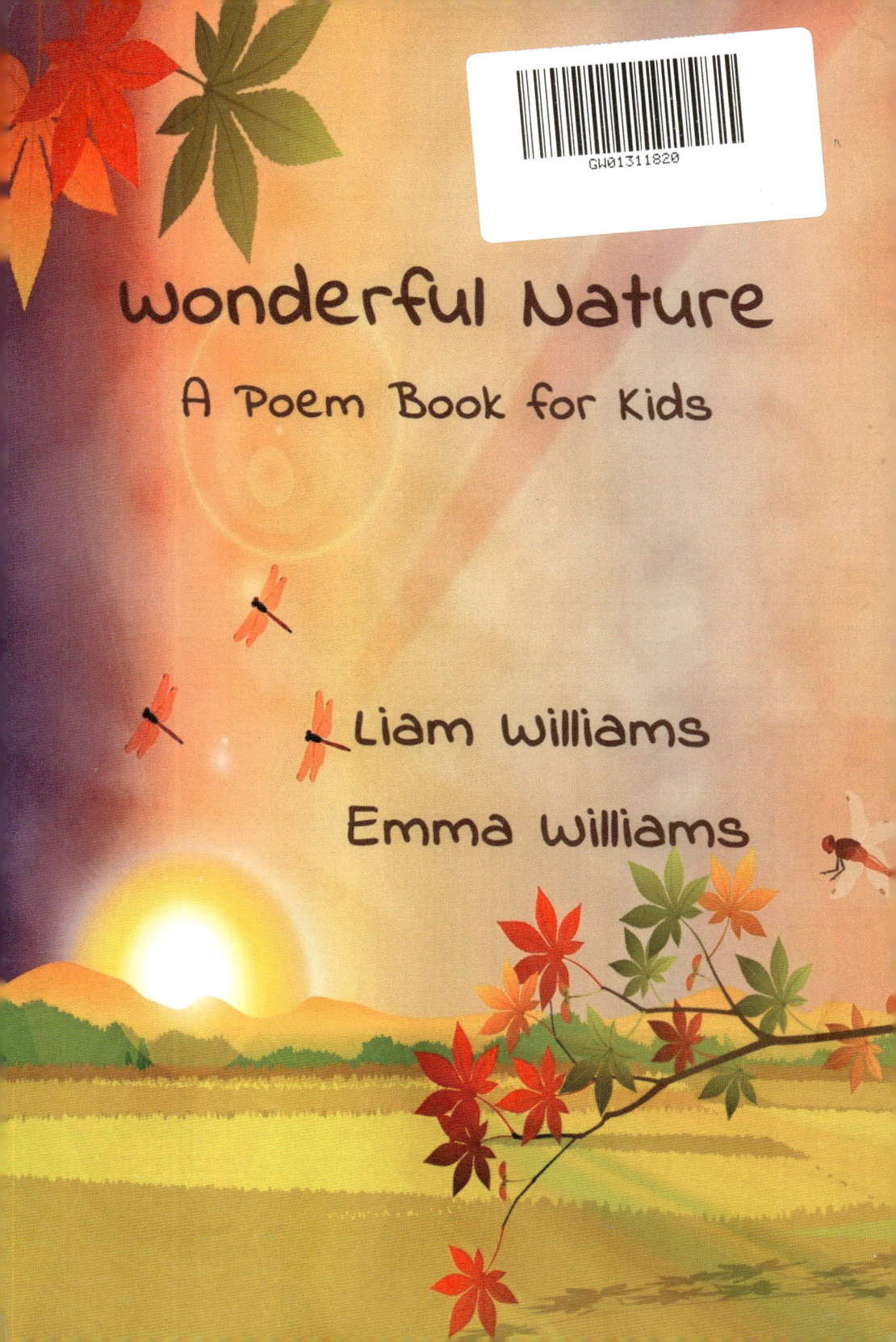

Wonderful Nature

A Poem Book for Kids

Liam Williams

Emma Williams

This page intentionally left blank

I am a planet in the solar system and my name is Earth.
Somewhere around 4.5 billion years ago lies my date of Birth.

Earth's surface is made up of clay, rocks and water and above them is the deep blue Sky.

Plants, animals, and humans live on the surface and in the skies, amazing birds Fly.

Earth's rotation about its axis causes
day and night.
Every twenty-four hours a new day
comes with fresh sunlight.

The Sun rises in the east
and sets in the west.
The Earth revolves around
the Sun and never takes rest.

Air is a mixture of many gases such
as oxygen and carbon dioxide.
Vital for both plants and animals, it
also helps the birds glide.

Rivers flow from high land to low
whether Mississippi or Nile.
They give us freshwater to drink and
make the soil fertile.

Sunlight and rain, plant and tree
make the Earth's air pollution free.

Just like animals in the forest we see, fishes and whales live in the sea.

Among all the minerals on Earth,
diamond is the hardest.
The highest point on Earth is
the Mount Everest.

Flowers are lively and they are colorful.

Colors come from light, isn't that wonderful.

High areas of lands are hills and mountains.
The sources of water are rivers and fountains.

In the winter,
weather is cold and it snows.

When summer comes,
temperature rises and hot air blows.

Below zero degree celsius, lakes'
surface turns into ice.
Under the ice in the lakes, fishes
survive, isn't it nice.

Trees give us fruits like mango, guava, and apple.
orange, red and yellow flowers grow on the tree of maple.

Sun and planets in the solar system, and stars everywhere. They are round in shape and look like sphere.

Sun shines during the day, moon is visible in the night.
The night sky appears dark and the stars are twinkling bright.

Plants use carbon dioxide and
sunlight to make healthy food.
They produce vegetables and fruits
which are tasty and good.

In winter water freezes, in
spring flowers grow.
Sunrays and rain combine to
form lovely rainbow.

Why plants are green, we wonder with zeal.
The green color comes from the pigment chlorophyll.

Plants give us refreshing tea and coffee. They also give us tasty chocolate and toffee.

Plants give us oxygen which keeps us alive.

They also give us healthy food so that we can thrive.

Freshwater is found in glaciers and rivers, salty is the water of ocean. Life in both land and ocean depend on energy of the sun.

The air we breathe gets refreshed
and purified by plants and trees.
Green vegetables are nutritious like
spinach, broccoli and peas.

Igneous, sedimentary and metamorphic are the three types of rocks.
They can be found in different forms, as small pieces or big blocks.

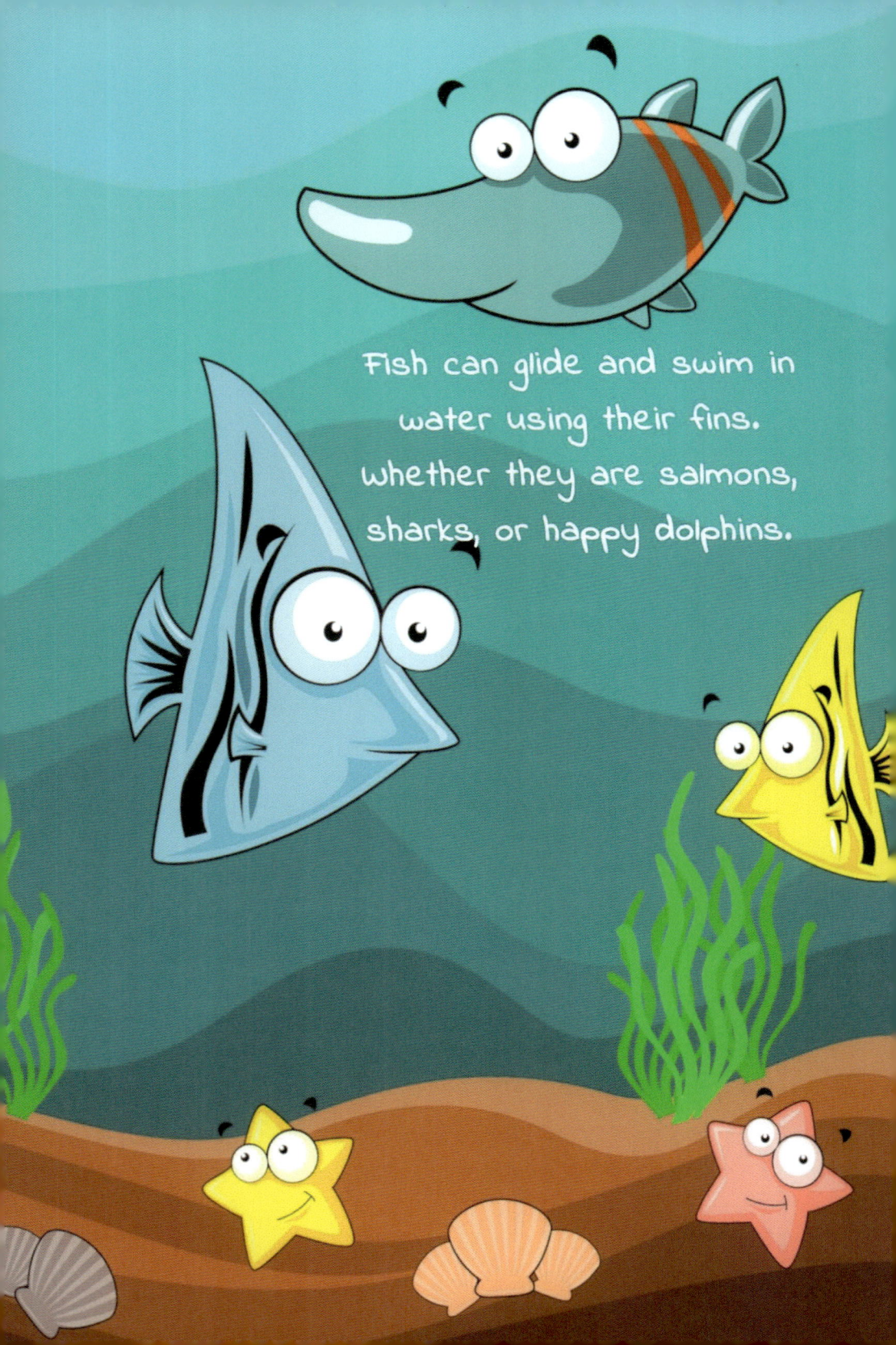

Fish can glide and swim in water using their fins. Whether they are salmons, sharks, or happy dolphins.

Some trees can grow more than
hundred meters high.
Birds can fly even higher several
miles in the sky.

Shrimp's heart is in its head,
octopus' hearts are three.
Life in sea is full of wonders and
quite a mystery.

Heat, light and sound are energy but in different forms.
we see and feel them in fire, lightning, and thunderstorms.

Adventurous and exciting is the safari
in a jungle.
Finding the right way in it is like
solving a jumble.

Some fruits are tangy, some fruits are sweet.
Whether oranges or mangoes, these are all nature's treat.

whether it's air, water or magnificent sunshine.

All these nature's gifts are great and sublime.

Penguins don't fly, but in icy cold water they dive.
A layer of fat on their body keeps them warm and alive.

Polar bear is a big animal which is found in the Arctic. Its fur is transparent but it appears white, isn't it fantastic.

NORTH POLE

Some clouds are high, some clouds are low.
Somewhere they rain, somewhere they snow.

The largest animals ever lived on earth
are the massive whales.
They live in the oceans and move their
body by flapping their tails.

Elephants are big and are heavy, deep forests are their home.
They have four pillar-like legs, in large wild fields they roam.

Sun

Mercury

Venus

Earth

Around the Sun, all planets revolve in the enormous space. Some planets move at very high speed, some at leisurely pace.

Mars

Jupiter

Neptune

Uranus

Saturn